PASSPORT to CAREER SUCCESS

Participant's Workbook

Ann Cross | Martha Lanaghen

CAREER SOLUTIONS

JIST

A DIVISION OF KENDALL HUNT

Minneapolis

Care has been taken to verify the accuracy of information presented in this book. However, the authors, editors, and publisher cannot accept responsibility for Web, email, newsgroup, or chat room subject matter or content, or for consequences from the application of the information in this book, and make no warranty, expressed or implied, with respect to its content.

Trademarks: Some of the product names and company names included in this book have been used for identification purposes only and may be trademarks or registered trade names of their respective manufacturers and sellers. The authors, editors, and publisher disclaim any affiliation, association, or connection with, or sponsorship or endorsement by, such owners.

We have made every effort to trace the ownership of all copyrighted material and to secure permission from copyright holders. In the event of any question arising as to the use of any material, we will be pleased to make the necessary corrections in future printings. Thanks are due to the aforementioned authors, publishers, and agents for permission to use the materials indicated.

ISBN 978-1-59357-971-5

Internet Resource Center: www.JIST.com/Passport

© 2015 by JIST Publishing, Inc., a division of Kendall Hunt
7900 Xerxes Avenue S STE 310
Minneapolis, MN 55431-1118
Email: service@jist.com
Website: JIST.com

Printed in the United States of America

CONTENTS

PREFACE

Whether you are actively seeking a job, looking to move up in your current organization, or simply exploring options for the future, you will find the information in this workbook and series of workshops helpful on your journey. *Passport to Career Success: Participant's Workbook* is intended to accompany workshops delivered by a career services professional. You will find the information in the workbook, and the variety of engaging tools included, to be a great guide on your exciting career path.

We have worked in the career services field for a combined 30 years. In that time, we have implemented dozens of training programs for colleges and universities, as well as within large corporations, and have spoken at many conferences. No matter where we are, we consistently hear employers asking for employees with stronger emotional intelligence and professionalism skills, rather than for employees with traditional "book learning" experiences. Career services professionals tell us that the lack of these soft skills (such as communication, problem solving, time management, and so on) is the greatest challenge job seekers must overcome as they begin a job search.

When you combine these valued soft skills with a savvy job search strategy, you are more likely to stay motivated throughout your search and to present yourself well in an interview—all of which will help you secure the job or promotion you desire.

Because so much has changed in the employment market in the last five years, searching for a new job can be confusing, but with the right tools, finding the right job can be easy. The *Passport to Career Success* program is designed to strengthen these critical soft skills and help you build the foundation for a successful job search.

The *Participant's Workbook* will provide you with helpful activities and challenges to support your participation in the *Passport to Career Success* workshops. The *Passport to Career Success* program includes eight compelling workshops to help you learn and master the important skills you need to become successfully employed:

1. **Social Media: Get Noticed and Get Hired**
   Learn how to create a personal brand and a professional online presence.

2. **Time Management: Budget Your Time and Get More Done**
   Learn highly productive habits that will lead to your success in the workplace.

3. **Professionalism: Unlock Your Potential with Soft Skills**
   Assess your own professionalism and set a course for building the skills and behaviors that will help you find a job and earn a promotion.

4. **Teamwork: Master the Art of Collaboration**
   Use teamwork to improve professional outcomes. Practice building teamwork skills and interacting successfully with your peers.

5. **Resume: Be Your Own Publicist**
   Collect the information you need to create an attention-grabbing resume and online profile.

6. **Job Search: Focus, Find, and Get the Job**
   Learn how to network and use the Internet to find and obtain your next job.

7. **Interviews: Present Your Best Self**
   Without a successful interview, you will not secure the job you want. Practice answering common interview questions and learn about interviewing do's and don'ts.

8. **Internships: Make Your Experience Count**
   Prepare for on-the-job learning experiences and learn the importance of the internship learning environment.

These workbooks include easy-to-use templates and practical tools to assist you with creating personalized job search tools that will help you present a professional image, identify great job openings, and successfully present your skills through resumes, social media, and interviews. When you attend the workshops, you will have the opportunity to practice new skills with your peers, as well as to learn from the expert facilitator.

PASSPORT to CAREER SUCCESS

SOCIAL MEDIA

Get Noticed and Get Hired

Worksheet 1: Create Your Personal Brand

Directions: Respond to the following questions to help identify your personal brand. Do not value-judge your answers. The key is to write down anything that comes to mind.

1. Describe yourself in a brief paragraph. Consider how you view yourself and how others may view you. What key ideas do you want associated with your image?

_____

_____

_____

_____

_____

_____

2. What are your areas of expertise? Every good brand has something that makes it stand out above the rest. What makes you stand out?

_____

_____

_____

_____

_____

_____

3. What does your style communicate to others? What do your nonverbal choices say about you? Consider the way you carry yourself, your clothing, your jewelry, and so on. Are you creative? Sloppy? Conservative?

_____

_____

_____

_____

_____

4. How would you like potential employers to think of you? Take two or three key words from each of the preceding questions and create a sentence that summarizes the personal brand that you want to create. Consider this your advertising slogan.

_____

_____

_____

Worksheet 2: Social Media Do's & Don'ts

With over one billion people using social networking sites such as Facebook, LinkedIn, and Twitter, social media has become an effective way to network and connect with other people. It is important to put forth an image that is aligned with the "brand" you have created for yourself. You will need to make certain that you are not posting any information on social media that does not align with your professional brand.

Identify Problem Areas

Consider the following recommendations when reviewing your own social media pages:

- Do not post anything you would not want an employer to see or know about you.
- Avoid any comments that could be interpreted as racist, sexist, or discriminatory in any way.
- Remove or untag photos that show you in an unfavorable light.
- Remove comments from your friends that seem distasteful (when in doubt, remove them!).
- Look at the apps on your profile. Does their purpose portray you well? If not, remove or hide them from view.
- Consider the groups you have joined. Do they align with your brand? If not, consider removing or hiding them from view or leaving the group.

Directions: Review the provided Facebook profile and identify 15 things that are wrong with the profile.

1. _____
2. _____
3. _____
4. _____
5. _____
6. _____
7. _____
8. _____
9. _____
10. _____
11. _____
12. _____
13. _____
14. _____
15. _____

Facebook Privacy Settings for Job Seekers

Make sure only _____ can see your photos.

Make sure only _____ can see your _____ and

_____ views.

Make sure only _____ can see your_____.

Facebook Privacy Settings

With the privacy settings, you are able to preview your site, a feature that will enable you to see what the outside world sees when visitors access your Facebook page. Check out these settings to ensure that employers can see only what you want them to see.

Carefully monitor who is tagging you on their posts and pictures to ensure you are not connected with unprofessional behavior or activities. Keep in mind that if you're being tagged in posts, employers may also see them depending on your privacy settings.

Note that other social media sites may have similar privacy options that you should examine.

Worksheet 3: LinkedIn Profiles

Benefits of a LinkedIn Profile

You can use LinkedIn as a tool to network and present your personal brand to employers online. Complete this worksheet to identify the benefits of creating a LinkedIn Profile and to brainstorm the information you can use within your profile. Use the following area to record information from the presentation.

In addition to having more than _____ users worldwide, LinkedIn allows you to do the following:

- _____ with _____ in your field (groups)
- Connect to _____
- Set up _____
- Conduct company _____
- Get _____
- Let company _____ find you
- Connect with _____
- Locate _____ jobs

One other benefit is that the _____ is right!

Analyze LinkedIn Profiles

Directions: Review the provided LinkedIn profile and answer the following questions.

1. What could be improved or fixed in the LinkedIn profile?

_____

_____

_____

_____

_____

_____

_____

_____

_____

2. What attributes should a profile picture possess?

_____

_____

_____

_____

_____

_____

_____

3. Do you have a profile picture that you could use for your own LinkedIn profile? If so, describe it here. If not, write down the steps you will take to obtain a suitable profile picture and set a deadline for yourself.

_____

_____

_____

_____

_____

_____

_____

Worksheet 4: Create Your Own Profile

Create a Headline

Recall that a headline is a way to grab others' attention and tell them something specific about yourself. Create your own headline by using some of the key words you brainstormed earlier. With these key words, create a headline for your profile. Good headlines are concise.

_____

_____

_____

_____

Create a Summary

A personal summary should clearly communicate your experience, expertise, and objectives. In the space below, write a first draft of your personal summary. You can start this process by inserting your "brand" sentence from Worksheet 1.

_____

_____

_____

_____

_____

_____

_____

_____

_____

_____

_____

Highlight Your Experience

Experience is a summary of your work history. You can download the information into LinkedIn directly from your resume or create it using the instructions on LinkedIn. A successful experience summary includes the following:

_____

_____

_____

_____

_____

Key Words Are Crucial

Incorporating well-rounded words throughout the experience section of your profile to describe strengths makes it easier for employers to find your profile and identify whether you are a good match for an open position.

LinkedIn profile key words such as *decisive*, *determined*, *productive*, and *steadfast* are all indicators of your professional abilities. Use key words like this throughout your LinkedIn profile, including in the headline, summary, and experience sections; and the skills section, too.

Your Experiences

Consider your past work, education, and life experiences and write down a brief list of these experiences. Within your list, highlight key words and related skills from these experiences.

- **Use related skills.** Try to find skills you have learned at your past jobs that are related to your new field.
- **Include unpaid experience if you have no work experience.** This is the place where volunteering, community service, and even extracurricular activities you have participated in will come into play.
- **Be honest.** Do not make up experience because employers will verify them for accuracy.

Other Languages

You will also increase your chance of getting an interview if you speak multiple languages. List any languages that you speak and write here:

Check Settings

Make sure your profile is public and that anyone can view it. Note that this is totally different from the privacy settings recommended for Facebook, where you want to limit public access. On LinkedIn, you *want* professionals to find you.

Connect with Others and Get Recommended

Consider whom you want to connect with and whom you could add to your network that may connect you to other employment opportunities. Write down the names of people you want to connect with and who may recommend you to others.

People to Connect with on LinkedIn	People to Ask for Recommendations

Worksheet 5: Self-Assessment of Social Media Skills

Directions: Try to accurately assess your social media skills and identify any areas for improvement. Using the following chart and rating scale, rate your use of social media based on what you learned today to assess your social media image and where you might improve your image. Use the last column to record your reason for selecting the rating that you did.

Rating Scale:

1. I don't use social media at all.

2. I have stuff on social media, but it has not necessarily been created with an employer in mind. Some might be inappropriate or not professional.

3. My social media sites are professional and carefully maintained so that I always present the best image to anyone that sees my sites.

Social Media Sites	Rate Yourself			Comments
Facebook	1	2	3	
LinkedIn	1	2	3	
Twitter	1	2	3	
Photo-sharing sites (Pinterest, Instagram, and so on.)	1	2	3	
Hobby or trade association sites	1	2	3	
Other sites	1	2	3	

Things I Can Do to Improve

For all the areas that you rated 1 or 2, identify two or three actions you can take to improve your rating. For those areas that you categorized as a 3, identify how you are utilizing the form of social media to benefit your job search. After completing this task, turn your work in to your workshop facilitator.

_____

_____

_____

_____

_____

_____

_____

_____

_____

_____

_____

Your Personal LinkedIn URL

If you have not created a LinkedIn profile, set aside some time to create a profile using the information you gathered in the previous handouts. Once you have a LinkedIn profile, record your personal LinkedIn URL below and send the link to your workshop instructor.

My personal LinkedIn URL:

_____

PASSPORT to CAREER SUCCESS

TIME MANAGEMENT

Budget Your Time and Get More Done

Worksheet 1: My Priorities

Directions: Identify your priorities by organizing them into the following groups.

My "Big Rocks"—The Really Important Stuff

(Examples: Education, family, work)

_____

_____

_____

_____

My "Marbles"—The Other Important Stuff

(Examples: Paying bills, exercising, commuting, making dinner)

_____

_____

_____

_____

My "Sand"—The Fun Stuff

(Examples: Hanging with friends, playing games, going to movies)

_____

_____

_____

_____

My "Water"—The Unexpected Stuff

(Examples: Car breaks down, child gets sick, a parent needs assistance)

_____

_____

_____

_____

Worksheet 2: How I Spend My Time

How I Spend My Time Now

Directions: Complete the following sections to identify the ways in which you spend your time.

1. I currently spend too much time on

_____
_____
_____
_____
_____
_____
_____

2. I currently don't spend enough time on

_____
_____
_____
_____
_____
_____
_____

Ways to Spend My Time More Wisely

You can do things to spend your time more wisely:

- Group similar activities together.
- Minimize interruptions for tasks that require focus.
- Make lists and prioritize items on the lists.
- Combine tasks/time requirements if you can.
- Create a "time budget" and stick to it.

Use the following space to record notes from the workshop as these methods are discussed.

_____

_____

_____

_____

_____

_____

_____

_____

_____

_____

_____

_____

_____

_____

_____

_____

_____

Group Similar Activities Together

Write down a few of the things that you need to get done each week. Then draw lines that connect the tasks that are similar and think about scheduling them back to back in the future.

_____   _____

_____   _____

_____   _____

_____   _____

_____   _____

Minimize Interruptions

Brainstorm a list of activities that would require your undivided attention and record them here along with a place you can go to focus on that particular task. Note any similar locations.

_____

_____

_____

_____

_____

_____

Make Priority Lists

Rewrite the list you created in Worksheet 1: My Priorities (what you need to get done each week), but organize the list so that the tasks are listed in order of importance. The first item on your list is what you consider the most important and the last item on the list is the least important.

1. _____
2. _____
3. _____
4. _____
5. _____
6. _____
7. _____
8. _____

9. _____
10. _____
11. _____
12. _____
13. _____
14. _____
15. _____
16. _____

Combine Tasks/Time Requirements

In the space provided, record some activities that you could complete at the same time. Think about things that happen in your day where you are waiting, and you could get other tasks done while you wait.

_____

_____

_____

_____

_____

Worksheet 3: Make a Time Budget

Create your own time budget using the provided time budget sample and time budget template. Feel free to make copies of the template to create your own time budget every week. The template has two sections:

1. A list of the week's priorities, an estimate of the time each task will require, and an estimate of when you expect to complete the task
2. A list of the days of the week and your priorities for the week

Time Budget Sample

The following is an example of a completed time budget. Use this sample as a guide to create your own time budget.

Activity	Deadline	Total Time Needed	When I Will Do This
Work.		40 hours	M, Tu, W, Th, F, 8–5
Update social networking.	By Friday	2 hours	Monday before dinner
Apply to at least two jobs.	Each week	1.5 hours	Tuesday after dinner and Sunday morning
Wash laundry and pay bills.	Thursday	2 hours	Thursday after dinner
Work out.		7 hours	Every day 6 a.m.

Sunday

Activity:	Work out.	Time allotted:	1 hour
Activity:	Cook meals for the week.	Time allotted:	3 hours
Activity:	Review job search websites.	Time allotted:	1.5 hours
Activity:		Time allotted:	

Monday

Activity:	Work out.	Time allotted:	1 hour
Activity:	Work.	Time allotted:	9 hours
Activity:	Update social networking.	Time allotted:	2 hours
Activity:		Time allotted:	

Time Budget Template

Activity	Deadline	Total Time Needed	When I Will Do This

Time Planner

Sunday

Activity: _____   Time allotted: _____

Activity: _____   Time allotted: _____

Activity: _____   Time allotted: _____

Activity: _____   Time allotted: _____

Monday

Activity: _____   Time allotted: _____

Activity: _____   Time allotted: _____

Activity: _____   Time allotted: _____

Activity: _____   Time allotted: _____

Tuesday

Activity: _____   Time allotted: _____

Activity: _____   Time allotted: _____

Activity: _____   Time allotted: _____

Activity: _____   Time allotted: _____

Wednesday

Activity: _____ Time allotted: _____

Activity: _____ Time allotted: _____

Activity: _____ Time allotted: _____

Activity: _____ Time allotted: _____

Thursday

Activity: _____ Time allotted: _____

Activity: _____ Time allotted: _____

Activity: _____ Time allotted: _____

Activity: _____ Time allotted: _____

Friday

Activity: _____ Time allotted: _____

Activity: _____ Time allotted: _____

Activity: _____ Time allotted: _____

Activity: _____ Time allotted: _____

Saturday

Activity: _____ Time allotted: _____

Activity: _____ Time allotted: _____

Activity: _____ Time allotted: _____

Activity: _____ Time allotted: _____

Notes

_____

_____

_____

_____

_____

PASSPORT to CAREER SUCCESS

PROFESSIONALISM

Unlock Your Potential with Soft Skills

Worksheet 1: Nonverbal, Get a Clue!

Directions: For each person/picture presented to you, answer the following questions in the space provided.

1. What kind of mood do you think this person is in?
2. How would you react to this person? Be descriptive.
3. How would this person make you feel if he or she responded to you with this body language and facial expression?

Picture 1

1. _____
2. _____
   _____
   _____
   _____
3. _____
   _____
   _____
   _____

Picture 2

1. _____
2. _____
   _____
   _____
   _____
3. _____
   _____
   _____
   _____

Picture 3

1. _____
2. _____
   _____
   _____
3. _____
   _____
   _____
   _____

Picture 4

1. _____
2. _____
   _____
   _____
3. _____
   _____
   _____
   _____

Picture 5

1. _____

2. _____

   _____

   _____

   _____

3. _____

   _____

   _____

   _____

   _____

Picture 6

1. _____

2. _____

   _____

   _____

   _____

3. _____

   _____

   _____

   _____

Worksheet 2: Key Components of Professionalism

Directions: Identify the seven keys to professionalism and analyze how they affect your job search by taking notes as you listen to the workshop.

Key Components of Professionalism

_____   _____

_____   _____

_____   _____

_____

Specialized Knowledge (Skill) Notes

- Acquired over _____, through _____
- Refreshed and _____ throughout your _____
- Learned in _____ by _____ other skilled professionals or through _____

Competency Notes

- Take good _____.
- Be _____ and _____.
- Ask _____ questions.
- Strive for _____ in your work.
- _____ your work for errors.
- Meet _____.
- Take _____ in your _____ communications.

Image Notes

- What you _____
- How you _____
- How you _____ yourself
- How you _____ yourself

Dressing for Success Notes

In the following space, record ideas from the brainstorming session about the do's and don'ts of professional dress.

Do's	Don'ts

Honesty and Integrity Notes

- Keep your _____.
- Do the _____ thing, even when it is _____.
- Be _____.
- Bc _____.
- Never speak _____ of your _____.
- Never participate in _____.
- Don't _____!

Accountability Notes

I demonstrate my professionalism when:

- I am accountable for my _____.
- I am accountable for my _____.
- I am accountable for my _____.

Other ways of demonstrating my professionalism include the following:

_____

_____

_____

_____

Positive Attitude Notes

- Leave your _____ at _____.
- Be _____ and _____.
- Stay _____ under _____.
- (Draw a picture of this one!) _____.

Self-Regulation Notes

- Practice good _____ management.
- Cut the _____ and do your work.
- Do not _____ the _____.
- Arrive _____ and stay _____.
- Minimize _____ and _____ time.
- Go _____ and _____.

What's in It for ME?

As a professional, I will:

_____

_____

_____

_____

_____

Worksheet 3: Self-Assessment of Professionalism Skills

Directions: Using the following scale, rate yourself based on what you learned in the Professionalism Workshop to assess your current professionalism practices. Then use the lower half of this page to identify your top priorities for improving your professionalism.

Professionalism Area	Until today, I did not even know this was important	I know about this but have a lot of work to do on this	I understand this and think I am OK at this
Specialized knowledge (skill in my profession)	1	2	3
My professional image	1	2	3
My honesty and integrity	1	2	3
My accountability	1	2	3
My competency	1	2	3
My positive attitude	1	2	3

Identify three of the professionalism skills that are your priorities for improvement, and write a few things you can do right away to improve:

- Area of focus: _____

  I will work on these: _____

  _____

  _____

  _____

- Area of focus: _____

  I will work on these: _____

  _____

  _____

  _____

- Area of focus: _____

  I will work on these: _____

  _____

  _____

  _____

PASSPORT to
CAREER SUCCESS

TEAMWORK
Master the Art of Collaboration

Worksheet 1: What Is a Team?

To What Teams Do You Belong?

Directions: To what teams do you belong? Brainstorm this question and record all possible answers in the following space. Add to this list as necessary.

What Does Every Great Team Have?

Directions: Complete the following sentences and answer the related questions based on the information presented in the Teamwork Workshop.

There are two primary roles on every great team: _____ and _____. Directors understand the team's _____, they understand what needs _____, and they understand the _____ of the team _____. Strong Directors will help to ensure that the team members are completing the _____ at the right _____ and that everyone is _____ together.

When have you been a Director?

_____

_____

_____

_____

_____

Doers understand the team's _____, they understand what needs _____, and they understand the job they need to complete for the team to be _____. Strong Doers will ensure that they complete the _____ at the right _____ and that they are _____ with their team.

When have you been a Doer?

_____

_____

_____

_____

_____

Directors spend most of their time directing _____. Doers spend most of their time directing _____.

Reflection Questions

1. Are you most often a Doer or a Director? (Circle one.)

   Doer   Director

2. Support your selection by listing a few examples of how you are a Doer or a Director in the space provided.

   _____

   _____

   _____

   _____

   _____

   _____

   _____

   _____

   _____

   _____

Worksheet 2: Self-Assessment — Am I a Great Team Member?

Directions: Complete the following sections using the information presented in the Teamwork Workshop.

Skill Area 1: Self-Awareness and Self-Control

When you are self-aware, you can _____ and set your _____ aside to work better as a team. You also _____ and _____. People who are self-aware also receive _____ very well and work to make changes and _____.

Ways to Improve Your Self-Control and Self-Awareness

- Ask for regular, open, and candid feedback from other team members.

- When they offer constructive criticism, say "thank you" and then think about what you can do to improve or address their concerns.

- Practice being aware "in the moment" when you want to react defensively to a situation. Force yourself to take a breath (literally count to five and breathe!).

Self-Assessment of Self-Control and Self-Awareness Skills

1. How would you rank your self-control and self-awareness? (Circle one.)

   Very Strong   Good   Needs Improvement

2. Explain why you chose that ranking.

   _____

   _____

   _____

3. In the following space, identify your action plan to improve your self-control and self-awareness.

   _____

   _____

   _____

   _____

   _____

   _____

   _____

Skill Area 2: Accountability and Responsibility

When you hold yourself accountable and take _____ for your actions, your team members can rely on you and good work _____ .
Being accountable and responsible means always _____ and doing it _____ .

Ways to Improve Accountability and Responsibility

- Do not procrastinate.
- Make task lists ("to-do lists") to help you organize your deliverables and stay on time.
- Use your calendar effectively. Block time to do your work, make sure you allow time for the unexpected, and aim to complete tasks early.
- Proofread and review your work to make sure it's accurate and of high quality. If you can, ask someone else to give you feedback before you deliver the final product to your boss.
- If you are going to miss a deadline, communicate with your team and work with your boss or peers to understand and minimize the impact of the delay.
- Offer to help other team members if they appear to need it.
- Ask for feedback and do your best to improve.

Self-Assessment of Accountability and Responsibility Skills

1. How would you rank your accountability and responsibility skills? (Circle one.)

   Very Strong   Good   Needs Improvement

2. Explain why you chose that ranking.

   _____

   _____

   _____

3. In the following space, identify your action plan to improve your accountability and responsibility.

   _____

   _____

   _____

   _____

   _____

   _____

   _____

   _____

Skill Area 3: Communication

The three important areas for great communication are _____,
_____ , and _____ .

Written communication includes _____ , _____ ,
and _____ .

Verbal communication is everything you _____ and how you interact
with _____ when they speak. _____ is a very
important part of verbal communication.

Asking great _____ is an important part of being a good communicator.
As a Doer, you need to _____ and to ask for
_____ when you're not sure. It's also important that
you ask your _____ if they need help and if they
_____ their responsibilities.

As a Director, you need to ask questions to make sure Doers _____ and
_____ .

Ways You Can Improve Your Communication Skills

- Proofread everything you send (emails, letters, documents) to make sure that it has the right tone, utilizes correct grammar and spelling, and accurately conveys what you mean. If possible, get someone else to review your work as well.

- Whenever issues are sensitive, speak directly with the person on the phone or in person; email can easily be misunderstood.

- As a rule of thumb, if a topic has taken more than three email exchanges, you should go directly to the person (on the phone or in person) to finalize the questions being considered.

- Practice active listening skills: paraphrase what you have heard to clarify understanding, focus on the speaker, and don't multitask.

- Take great notes. Doing so not only improves your memory but also gives you a record of key outcomes from meetings or conversations. Always carry a notebook and pen or pencil, and make notes in every meeting.

- Sometimes you have to be brave to ask good questions. As a Doer or a Director, make sure your colleagues, peers, and direct reports understand their tasks and feel safe asking questions. When you're not sure, it's far better to ask for clarification than to do the wrong thing well. Practice asking good questions!

Self-Assessment of Communication Skills

1. How would you rank your communication skills? (Circle one.)

   Very Strong   Good   Need Improvement

2. Explain why you chose that ranking.

   _____

   _____

   _____

3. In the following space, identify your action plan to improve your communication skills.

_____

_____

_____

_____

_____

_____

_____

Skill Area 4: Give Praise, Share the Blame—Being Part of a Great Team

When great things happen, be sure to give _____ to your coworkers.

Be specific about _____ and _____.

When things go wrong, ask yourself first,

_____ Then ask,

_____ Even if the

situation wasn't your _____, take _____ and

describe how you will _____.

Ways You Can Improve Your Teamwork Skills

1. Every time something is behind schedule or not up to quality standards, think of how you could help to improve the schedule and then take action.

2. When your teammates do great things, even when they are small things, get in the habit of saying something specific and kind to let them know you noticed. Better yet, write down your thoughts and give them a little written "pat on the back."

3. When you are praised for something, make sure you acknowledge anyone else who helped you to be successful.

4. Remember that it is more important to get good things done than it is to get credit or praise for getting them done.

Self-Assessment of Teamwork Skills

1. How would you rank your teamwork skills? (Circle one.)

Very Strong   Good   Need Improvement

2. Explain why you chose that ranking.

_____

_____

_____

3. In the following space, identify your action plan to improve how you give praise and share blame.

_____

_____

_____

_____

_____

_____

_____

_____

_____

_____

Apply the Concepts

Answer the following questions using the information you just learned:

1. Think of a time when something went wrong and describe the problem.

_____

_____

_____

_____

2. How did you respond to the situation (if at all)?

_____

_____

_____

_____

_____

_____

_____

_____

_____

3. How *should* you have responded to the situation?

_____

_____

_____

_____

_____

_____

_____

_____

_____

4. Consider all the ways you could have prevented the problem from happening (even if it wasn't your fault). Record these actions to identify ways you could make sure the problem doesn't happen again.

_____

_____

_____

_____

_____

_____

_____

_____

_____

_____

PASSPORT to
CAREER SUCCESS

RESUME

Be Your Own Publicist

Worksheet 1: Resume Comparisons

Directions: Read Bob Smith's resume (Figure 5.1) on page 48. Take a moment to read the resume, and look at the formatting and content. Then in the space below, make notes about what you like and don't like about the resume.

_____

_____

_____

_____

_____

_____

Refer to Larry Jones's resume (Figure 5.2) on page 49. Take a moment to read the resume, and look at the formatting and content. Then in the space below, make notes about what you like and don't like about the resume.

_____

_____

_____

_____

_____

Compare Larry's resume to Bob's resume. Then in the space below, make notes about what you like and don't like about Larry's resume in relation to Bob's. Would you hire Larry or Bob? Why?

_____

_____

_____

_____

_____

_____

Bob Smith
1234 Main Street
My Town, TN 60612

Job Objective

To get hred in a position at a doctor's office or medical clinic in my hometown, as a medical assistant after I graduate from college.

Work Experience

Wal-Mart, Hometown, TN—June 2000 to present

I am the lead cashier on the morning shift at the local Wal-Mart. I greet customers, scan and checkout groshries and merchandize. I used to be the stock clerk in housewars then I got promoted because of my attendance record and good customer service.

YMCA of MyTown, MyTown, TN—June to August 1997, 1998, and 1999

Summer camp counsiler. I worked with kids from age 5 to 15 at the basketball camp and outdoor sports camp. I was a counsilor in 1997, and lead basketball counsilor in 1998 and 1999. I had to schedule the other counsilors, check equipment, keep track of the kids, talk to parents and work with the other YMCA staff.

Education

Graduated from MyTown Valley High School, May 1998

Attending MyTown Business and Medical College currently

Personal

I'm a dedicated and hard worker with very good attendance at school and I've been working on my family ranch since I was 8. I like to ride horses, was the captin of my high school football team, and play golf.

Figure 5.2: Larry's Resume

LARRY JONES

9876 Broadway Drive ♦ My Town, TN 60612
987-654-3210 ♦ LarryJones1@pass.emcp.com
www.linkedin.com/in#/LarryJones#1

JOB OBJECTIVE

Looking for opportunity to contribute to a medical office team in a Medical Assistant role that will leverage over 10 years of customer service experience and my college coursework in Medical Assistance

SKILLS SUMMARY

Customer Service—over 7 years' experience in positions that required direct work with customers, recognized for delivering excellent customer care. *Completed Conflict Resolution 1* and *Conflict Resolution 2, Telephone Etiquette* and *Dealing with Difficult Customers* workshops

Attention to Detail—experience working with cash drawers, and filing systems that required rapid completion of detailed tasks with high degree of accuracy

Teamwork and Collaboration—member of high-performance teams where working closely on tasks was required for successful completion of projects; Positive attitude and open communication style

Communication—good written and verbal communication skills including good grammar and typing as well as ability to communicate verbally individually, and in small groups; Comfortable presenting to small- and medium-sized audiences.

Flexible—ability to work days, evenings and weekends; Own reliable transportation and can commute to branch locations if required.

Hard Working—demonstrated ability to work long hours, seek new knowledge and adapt to changing situations with ease.

WORK HISTORY

Wal-Mart, Hometown, TN—November 2010 to present—*Automotive Department Stock Clerk*

Gas-n-Drive, Anytown, TN—October 2008 to August 2010—*Cashier and Customer Service*

TechSupport USA, MyTown, TN—January 2006 to January 2008—*Technical Support Representative*

Summer of Fun Camps, MyTown, TN—Summers 2003 to 2005—*Camp Counselor*

EDUCATION

- Graduated from HomeTown High School, May 2005
- MyTown Business and Medical College, Expected Graduation—Fall 2012
  Associate Degree Medical Assisting

Worksheet 2: Notes for Writing a Winning Resume

Six Keys to Resume Success

1. _____—Use _____ space and easy-to-read _____. Keep important information _____. Use _____ points.

2. **Typos and grammatical errors**—Do not make them! _____ carefully. Better yet, get a _____ to _____ your resume and cover letter, too!

3. **Contact information**—Place information at the _____. Make sure it is complete and _____.

4. **Write PAR (Problem, Action, _____) statements**—When you can, use specific _____ for results.

5. _____ **key words**—Use active verbs and nouns.

6. **Organization**—Use _____-based , chronological, or _____ format.

Worksheet 3: Bob's Revised Resume

Figure 5.3: Bob's Revised Resume

BOB SMITH

123-456-1234 ♦ bobsmith@pass.emcp.com
www.linkedin.com/in#/BobSmith#1

JOB OBJECTIVE: Seeking opportunity as a Medical Assistant that will leverage my proven customer service skills and dependability in an exciting and busy medical environment

WORK EXPERIENCE

Wal-Mart, Hometown, TN—June 2000 to Present

Promoted to *Lead Cashier,* October 2007

- Identified that scheduling practices hurt employee morale; partnered with two other lead cashiers to develop new shift-bidding system; reduced cashier turnover by 25 percent by implementing the new system
- Supervised all activities throughout my shifts
- Selected to attend regional team building training and to implement team building program at our Wal Mart store

Promoted to *Cashier,* May 2003 to October 2007

- Delivered outstanding customer service for all checkout transactions

Stock Clerk—Housewares, June 2000 to May 2003

- Reviewed inventory reports and re-stocked shelves based on expected sales
- Improved cleanliness ratings within my department by 4 points in first year

YMCA of MyTown, MyTown, TN—*Summer Camp Counselor,* Summers 1997, 1998, and 1999

- Promoted to lead counselor after first summer season
- Created schedule for all basketball camps
- Supervised children and junior counselors
- Identified 12 key safety risk areas; attended a YMCA safety and risk training session and implemented a new safety and security assurance program; helped the summer camp stay accident-free for two consecutive years

EDUCATION

Graduated from MyTown Valley High School, May 1998

MyTown Business and Medical College, Expected Graduation—Fall 2012
Associate Degree Medical Assisting

AWARDS

- Perfect Attendance 8 terms out of 12— MyTown Business and Medical College
- Wal-Mart Excellent Customer Care Award, Fall 2008

Resume Analysis

Directions: Compare Bob's new resume to the old resume found in Worksheet 1. How has the resume been improved? Record your observations in the space below and consider the question of whom you would like to hire—Bob (based on his new resume) or Larry?

_____

_____

_____

_____

_____

_____

_____

_____

_____

_____

_____

_____

Worksheet 4: Types of Resumes & Resume Components

Three Types of Resumes

Use a chronological or time-based resume in these situations:

_____

_____

_____

Use a skills-based resume in these situations:.

_____

_____

_____

Use a combination time- and skills-based resume in these situations:.

_____

_____

_____

The Five Resume Components

1. _____
2. _____
3. _____
4. _____
5. _____

Worksheet 5: Resume Template

Directions: Identify the individual components that you will use in your own resume by filling out the following information. When you are done, you can take the information from this template directly into a computer document or online job application to create your resume. Remember to format your resume using what you have learned so that it is clear and easy to follow.

Contact Information

Name: _____

Telephone/email: _____

LinkedIn account URL: _____

Job Objective

_____

_____

Skills

_____

_____

_____

_____

_____

_____

_____

Work Experience

Most recent (or current) job (company and title): _____

Bullet points about my work—use active verbs and PAR (problem, action, results) statements:

_____

_____

_____

_____

_____

_____

_____

Prior job (company and title): _____

Bullet points about my work—use active verbs and PAR (problem, action, results) statements:

_____
_____
_____
_____
_____
_____
_____
_____
_____
_____

Education / Awards

_____
_____
_____
_____
_____
_____
_____
_____
_____
_____
_____
_____

References

Reference name: _____

Type of reference (personal, professional, academic, other): _____

Contact information: _____

This person has given me permission to use him or her as a reference: _____ YES / NO

Reference name: _____

Type of reference (personal, professional, academic, other): _____

Contact information: _____

This person has given me permission to use him or her as a reference: _____ YES / NO

Reference name: _____

Type of reference (personal, professional, academic, other): _____

Contact information: _____

This person has given me permission to use him or her as a reference: _____ YES / NO

Examples of how you might list your references on your resume:

Maria Smythe
Former Supervisor at USA Merchandise Mart
555-111-1212
Msmythe@pass.emcp.com

William Franklin
Pastor at First Church
555-444-1234
bfrank@pass.emcp.com

Worksheet 6: Cover Letter Exercise

Directions: Read the following job advertisement and then examine the cover letter samples on the following pages. What do you see that you like? What could be improved? Record your analysis in the space provided on page 61.

Job Advertisements

Figure 5.4: Advertisement 1

MEDICAL ASSISTANT—EXPERIENCE PREFERRED

If you have attention to detail and excellent interpersonal skills and are willing to work evenings and weekends, we are looking for you! The ideal candidate will have experience working in a busy environment and will be reliable. Our patients have come to know us as a highly caring, convenient, patient-oriented clinic. We are **HomeTown Family Practice** with locations around the metro area.

The successful candidate will earn a competitive salary and a benefits package that includes medical, dental, and vacation. Please submit your resume to Maria Tucker at 1234 Broadway, Hometown, AK 12345.

Cover Letter Components

A cover letter is your first means of introduction to a potential employer. Each cover letter has four important components:

- **Header and salutation.** The header includes the recipient's name, title, physical address, and the date that you are writing the letter. If you do not know the recipient's physical address, leave that blank.
- **Introduction.** In the first paragraph, answer the following questions:
  - Who are you?
  - What are you applying for?
  - Where did you learn about the job?
  - Why do you want the job? Tell the hiring manager you are serious about getting the job!

- **Summary of your qualifications.** In a second paragraph, explain your qualifications and make sure they are tailored to the job description or advertisement. (Do not be shy!)
- **Thank you and closing.** In a brief closing paragraph, include the following:
  - Thank the recipient for considering you.
  - Refer the recipient to your resume for additional information.
  - Reiterate your interest in the position.
  - Include your phone number and email address so someone can immediately contact you if desired.

Use a professional and friendly closing salutation, such as "Best regards," "Kind regards," or "Sincerely."

Miss Maggie Stover
198 Oak Street
MyTown, AK 12345
555-345-2345

[Date]

Miss Maria Tucker
1234 Broadway Street
Hometown, AK 12345

Dear Ms. Tucker,

I am writing in regard to your job posting, titled *Medical Assistant—Experience Preferred,* that was featured on Monster.com. Please accept my enclosed resume as a summary of my applicable experience. Given my proven record of effective work in busy clinical environments, I believe I will be an excellent addition to the **HomeTown Family Practice** team.

My background includes a breadth of experience in customer service and patient care roles. Additionally, I am able to work evenings and weekends and my supervisors will tell you that my work ethic, attention to detail, and reliability are second to none.

I am excited about the prospect of working in an environment where patient care and convenience are important, and I am particularly interested in the position you have posted because it presents an opportunity to work with a variety of patients and to acquire new skills and knowledge.

I also want to assure you that I have reliable transportation and the ability to work at your three branch locations, or any new locations that you open within the greater HomeTown market.

Thank you in advance for reviewing my credentials for your open position. I look forward to hearing from you regarding next steps.

Sincerely,

Maggie Stover

Maggie Stover
Enclosure: Resume

Figure 5.6: Advertisement 2

PROJECT MANAGEMENT ASSISTANT

We are the area's leading insurance agency specializing in a diverse product mix so we can serve our customers' personal and business insurance needs. We are getting ready to expand our business and are looking for an entry-level project manager assistant.

Must be proficient with all MS Office tools including MS Excel, MS Word, and PowerPoint; as well as being proficient computer user with the ability to conduct online research.

The ideal candidate will have the ability to learn quickly, and will be creative. He/she will work effectively with teams and be a self-starter who can figure out what needs to be done next and then get it done. Please submit resumes to Bill Franklin, VP of Projects, at 3345 Strawberry Street, MyTown, NY 33245.

Mr. Pat Blake
13434 Sycamore Street
Broadville, NY 94857
555-546-1235

[Date]

Mr. Bill Franklin
Vice President of Projects
3345 Strawberry Street
MyTown, NY 33245

Dear Mr. Franklin,

I am pleased to present my credentials for the position you posted on CareerBuilder.com entitled *PROJECT MANAGEMENT ASSISTANT*.

I am excited by the prospect of working for a company that is growing and in which rapid change is the norm. My experience has made me uniquely prepared to succeed in such an environment. My skills include the following:

- Advanced user of MS Excel and Word, proficient user of MS PowerPoint
- Proficient computer user including extensive online research experience using Google and other research tools, as well as other tools such as Dropbox, LexisNexis, and Hoovers.com
- Demonstrated ability to learn quickly and adapt to new environments as illustrated by my rapid promotion at my current job
- Self-directed employee with the ability to partner effectively with cross-functional team members, as well as external vendors and stakeholders
- Some experience supervising workers
- Completed project management coursework as part of my degree in business

I am eager to grow and learn with the right company and appreciate the time you are taking to consider my application. I look forward to hearing from you regarding next steps.

Best regards,

Pat Blake

Pat Blake
Attachment: Resume

Cover Letter Analysis

Cover Letter 1

Cover Letter 2

Worksheet 7: Practice Writing a Cover Letter

Locate and Identify a Potential Job

Look online or in the paper and identify a job that you think you would like to apply for now or in the future. You will always want to tailor your cover letters to each job, so it is essential that you know the name of the company and what that company is seeking in a candidate before you create your cover letter. Identify the following information about the job you have found to use for this exercise:

- Name of company: _____
- Job title: _____
- Required/requested skills and education: _____

_____

_____

_____

_____

Cover Letter Components

Directions: Use the following worksheet to identify information that you would use in your own cover letter. This information can be saved to use as a guide for future cover letters.

Header/Salutation

_____

_____

_____

Introduction

Be sure to answer the following questions in your introduction:

- Who are you?
- What are you applying for?
- Where did you learn about the job?
- Why do you want the job? Tell the recipient you are serious about getting the job.

_____

_____

_____

_____

_____

Summary of Your Qualifications

Refer to the job posting and information you noted in the first part of this worksheet for ideas about how to present your experience and how to emphasize the skills the job requires. Remember to write PAR statements whenever possible.

_____

_____

_____

_____

_____

_____

_____

_____

_____

Thank You and Closing

_____

_____

_____

_____

Create Your Cover Letter

Now you have all the components of a great cover letter. Use this information as a guide for the creation of your future cover letters. You will need to create a new cover letter for each job to which you apply. Take what you have written and format it using your favorite word processing software. When it is available, you can attach it electronically to your resume, upload it to application websites, or print it to accompany your resume when you apply in person or attend an interview.

PASSPORT to CAREER SUCCESS

JOB SEARCH

Focus, Find, and Get the Job

Worksheet 1: Know What You Want!

Assess Your Strengths and Interests

Directions: Consider what you have liked and not liked about previous employment or activities. Use your own experiences to answer the following questions in the space provided.

1. What did/do I like best about my past or current job(s)?

_____

_____

_____

_____

_____

2. What did/do I enjoy doing most in school?

_____

_____

_____

_____

_____

3. What are some areas where I feel particularly skilled and capable?

_____

_____

_____

_____

_____

4. What are my goals?

_____

_____

_____

_____

_____

_____

Identify Your Ideal Job

Directions: Based on the information you identified in the first section, write down a few sentences about the job that you want. It should be a job that you think is the best fit for your abilities and personality. This is your "ideal" job. For example, "My ideal job will allow me schedule flexibility and the opportunity to supervise people."

_____

_____

_____

_____

If you know specific job titles that align with your explanation of the ideal job, write them down. If not, make a list of attributes of the job and the skills you will use.

Specific Job Titles

_____

_____

_____

Attributes of Your Ideal Job

_____

_____

_____

_____

Skills You Will Use at Your Ideal Job

_____

_____

_____

Research Your Ideal Jobs

Great resources for job title research:

- O*Net (www.oNetOnline.org/skills)
- www.MySkillsMyFuture.org
- www.Monster.com
- www.CareerBuilder.com
- www.Indeed.com
- www.Jobing.com

Make a List of Target Companies

Directions: Using the Internet or business section of the newspaper, identify the companies that currently employ people in the job you have identified as your ideal job. Include companies that may not have current job openings. The goal is to identify your ideal employers so you can monitor their employment opportunity announcements and learn what you need to do to qualify for their positions. List as many companies as you can in the space provided.

1. _____
2. _____
3. _____
4. _____
5. _____
6. _____
7. _____
8. _____
9. _____
10. _____
11. _____
12. _____
13. _____
14. _____
15. _____
16. _____
17. _____
18. _____
19. _____
20. _____
21. _____
22. _____
23. _____
24. _____
25. _____
26. _____
27. _____
28. _____
29. _____
30. _____

Worksheet 2: Create a Great Elevator Speech

A great elevator speech has three important components:

1. A concise and specific statement about _____ that features your _____ or background

2. A powerful statement about _____ to show evidence that you will be a _____

3. A concise statement about the _____, including appropriate _____

Write your elevator speech here:

_____

_____

_____

_____

_____

_____

_____

_____

_____

_____

Consider incorporating content from your elevator speech into the following:

- _____
- _____
- _____
- _____
- _____
- _____

Worksheet 3: Market Yourself

What Is a "Good-Fit" Job?

1. A job for which I am _____

2. A job that meets my _____ and _____ needs

3. A job at a company that I _____

Where to Look?

_____

_____

_____

_____

_____

LinkedIn

LinkedIn is a powerful tool in your job search:

- Use LinkedIn's automated feature to _____ address book and

  _____.

- Connect to as _____ people as possible, but remember, these are

  _____ connections, so don't post and chat with people as you would

  on Facebook.

- Use a _____. Spend the money to have one taken if you don't have a

  good one to use.

- Complete every part of the _____, including skills.

- Write _____ for your colleagues and connections, and

  _____ them to recommend you.

- _____ others for their skills. This will encourage them to endorse

  you in return. Note, however, that you should endorse only skills that you know are accurate

  representations of your contact.

- Add professional status _____.

- Join _____ that are pertinent to your job search and your career, participate

  in their _____, and watch their _____ for

  listings and other possible connections.

Worksheet 4: Resume Submission Tracker

Directions: Use this document to record all the companies to which you submitted your resume. You can find additional copies on the Internet Resource Center (IRC).

Website/Company Name (URL if website)	User Name	Password (or Password Reminder)	Date Resume Posted	Date Cover Letter Posted	Comments

Worksheet 5: Networking Tracker

Directions: Use this document to record the names of new people you add to your network. Be sure to include the name of the company for which they work and how you are connected with them. You can find additional copies on the Internet Resource Center (IRC).

Networking Tracker							
Networking Event	Date	Acquaintance Name/Title	Company Name	Contact Email Address	Contact Phone Number	Comments	

Worksheet 6: Career Website Tracker

Directions: Use this document to record all the websites you have used as you search for jobs. This way, you can keep track of the different websites you may have joined during your job search. Note that it's not wise to write down passwords. Consider adding a password hint to column 3 instead of recording each of the passwords you create during your search. You can find additional copies on the Internet Resource Center (IRC).

Career Website Tracker				
Website	User Name	Password (or Password Reminder)	Focus of the Website	Comments

Worksheet 7: Interview Tracker

Directions: Use this document to record information about interviews you have obtained and completed. As you continue your job search, you'll find it can be difficult to keep track of all the details. This document will help you make sure you follow up appropriately with thank you notes and that you remember important information from each interview that may be helpful in your job search. You can find additional copies on the Internet Resource Center (IRC).

Interview Tracker							
Company	Date	Interviewer Name/Title	Contact/Email Address	Contact Phone Number	Date Follow-Up	Date "Thank You" Sent	Comments

Worksheet 8: Job Search Checklist

Use the following checklist to assist you in your job search. You can find additional copies of this checklist on the Internet Resource Center (IRC).

- [ ] I have created my LinkedIn profile, and it is as complete as possible.
- [ ] I have added my elevator speech in appropriate places:
    - [ ] LinkedIn profile
    - [ ] Resume
    - [ ] Facebook page
    - [ ] Business card
- [ ] I have reviewed my resume for accuracy.
- [ ] I have signed up with _____ (#) staffing agencies.
- [ ] I have changed my ring tone and voicemail messages to be professional.
- [ ] I have discussed the importance of answering the phone professionally with anyone that might answer my phone (family, housemates, and so on).
- [ ] I have prepared my email to inform my network that I am looking for a job.
- [ ] I have researched where the job workforce center posts information about job fairs.
- [ ] I have practiced answering the phone.
- [ ] I have searched online using my key words and targeted the following jobs/companies:

1) _____

2) _____

3) _____

4) _____

5) _____

6) _____

7) _____

8) _____

☐ I have searched online using my key words and targeted the following job titles. (Most job search engines will let you create and save your favorite searches. Be sure to save a search with each of the job titles you've identified below.)

1) _____

2) _____

3) _____

4) _____

5) _____

6) _____

7) _____

8) _____

PASSPORT to CAREER SUCCESS

INTERVIEWS

Present Your Best Self

Worksheet 1: Nonverbal Cues

Complete this activity to demonstrate and identify how nonverbal messages can influence others as much as the words we speak.

Directions: With a partner and using only facial expressions and body language, practice displaying the emotions listed here. Take turns with each set of emotions. When you are finished, write an analysis that judges the applicant based on these nonverbal cues.

Applicant 1: Negative Nonverbal

1. Annoyed/Irritated
2. Sleepy
3. Shy
4. Impatient
5. Sad

Applicant 2: Positive Nonverbal

1. Happy
2. Interested
3. Relaxed/Comfortable
4. Confident
5. Calm

Analysis

Applicant 1

_____

_____

_____

_____

Applicant 2

_____

_____

_____

_____

Worksheet 2: POW! Powerful Answers to Interview Questions

Three Types of Interview Questions

Directions: In the following spaces, identify the three types of interview questions that your facilitator describes. Below each one, add your notes about what each type includes:

1. Type of Question: _____

   Examples: _____

   _____

   _____

   _____

   _____

2. Type of Question: _____

   Examples: _____

   _____

   _____

   _____

   _____

3. Type of Question: _____

   Examples: _____

   _____

   _____

   _____

   _____

   _____

POWerful! Interview Responses

When you are asked questions in an interview, you want to convey your answers in a concise, thoughtful way that focuses on action and results. POW! is a great way to practice being concise and not rambling through your answers.

P = Preview

O = Our actions or **Our** attitudes

W = What happened? or **what** that means to my work? So **what**!

1. The _____ should tell someone in a _____ what you did or what you think—a _____ of your answer.

2. Our _____—this is where you explain _____ you feel the way you do or what you _____ to get a _____ .

3. The "so what?" explains what the _____ was of your actions or what _____ your feelings have on your _____ .

Examples of Common Questions and POW!

Question

What are your strengths in the workplace? (This is an "actions" question.)

Answer

Preview—My supervisor told me I am very good at problem solving.

Our Action/Attitude—When we saw a decline in sales, I created a spreadsheet that analyzed our advertising and identified that three media outlets were not performing. We canceled those outlets and tested three new outlets.

So What—The result was that our spending increased 3 percent, but our response increased 10 percent and sales began to rise again.

Question

Describe the ideal boss. (This is a "feelings" or "opinions" question.)

Answer

Preview—The ideal boss will challenge me to learn new things.

Our Actions/Attitudes—I'm the happiest and most productive when I am challenged and learning…

So What— …and that will make me more valuable to my team and the company.

Worksheet 3: Ten Most-Asked Interview Questions

Common Interview Questions

Following are common interview questions that job applicants should be ready to answer during a job interview. You won't necessarily see all of them, and they may or may not be in this order, but you can use this list to practice POWerful answers and prepare for your interview.

1. Please tell us about yourself.
2. Why are you the best candidate for the job?
3. Why are you interested in our company or this position?
4. Why did you leave your last job? OR Why do you want to leave your current job?
5. What is your greatest weakness?
6. Tell me about a time you faced an obstacle and what you did to overcome it.
7. What was the most frustrating experience you had at your last job, and what was the most satisfying experience?
8. How have you handled angry customers or peers?
9. What are your salary expectations?
10. Do you have any questions?

Practicing POW!

Directions: Record your own answers to the questions that follow. Feel free to write detailed answers or write general phrases and notes that you can use later when practicing for an interview. For those questions that may require knowledge about the employer, do your own research on an employer you would like to work for and answer the questions accordingly. Use the POW! approach in your answer. Question 1 includes the three steps of POW!, but you should apply them to the remaining nine questions also.

1. **Please tell us about yourself.**

   This question often sets the stage for the entire interview. When answering, include the overall message that you want to leave with the employer as well as your most recent accomplishments. Finish with an explanation of why you want to work for the company.

   • **Step 1:** Using the "POW!" approach, build your opening line for this question.

   _____

   _____

   _____

   • **Step 2:** In no more than three sentences, write the Our Actions/Attitude paragraph to the answer.

   _____

   _____

   _____

   _____

- **Step 3:** In one sentence, summarize your answer and make your statement impactful!

_____

_____

- **Step 4:** Using the answer you just wrote, role-play your answer with your partner if possible. Ask for feedback and make any notes about areas for improvement.

_____

_____

_____

_____

2. **Why are you the best candidate for the job?**

When you are answering this question, having confidence is essential. This answer should leave the interviewer with the impression that you are confident, calm, and capable. Emphasize the qualities you possess that align with the company culture. A good answer will consist of "In conducting my research on your company, I found ... and I possess ... which I believe aligns with (*job description facts*), making me the best candidate."

_____

_____

_____

_____

_____

_____

3. **Why are you interested in our company or this position?**

This question is your chance to show the interviewer that you have done your homework! Use your response as an opportunity to get a leg up on your competition by talking about the company motto or mission statement and how you feel personally aligned with that mission.

_____

_____

_____

_____

_____

_____

4. Why did you leave your last job OR why do you want to leave your current job?

Above all else, honesty is the most important piece of your answer. The next is never disparaging your former employer or coworkers. Always present your current and past coworkers in a positive light; otherwise, the interviewer may question your ability to work as a cooperative team member.

_____

_____

_____

_____

_____

_____

_____

5. What is your greatest weakness?

This question can be tricky to answer correctly. Answering this question has become somewhat cliché because people are taught to say things that are really positive such as "I am a perfectionist" or "I spend too much time at the office." The best way to answer this question is to be honest about your weakness, but to acknowledge to the interviewer that you are aware of the weakness and are working on it. An example might be "I'm told I could be more direct, so I regularly ask for feedback after I've expressed a concern or raised an issue on a project, and that is helping me to clarify and practice being more direct" or "I need to work on my public speaking. I've made an effort to volunteer for more public speaking assignments. I'm still nervous, but I'm getting better and better every time."

_____

_____

_____

_____

_____

_____

_____

6. **Tell me about a time you faced an obstacle and what you did to overcome it.**

When you are answering this question, keeping your answer related to your profession is key. Often candidates will use examples from their personal life or use examples about conflicts they had with coworkers. Neither is a good idea. The interviewer is looking at your problem-solving and critical-thinking abilities, so use an example in which you used quick thinking and independence to solve a problem related to your work.

7. **What was the most frustrating experience you had at your last job, and what was the most satisfying experience?**

When answering this question, make sure your response includes how your own actions may have contributed to the problem. Taking personal responsibility is important. For example, saying "No one else worked as hard as I did" means that you see things only from your perspective. A better answer would be "At times, the group I worked with lacked the teamwork necessary to operate at our highest capacity." When you answer a question about your most satisfying experience, be sure to credit any teamwork that might have helped the experience but also highlight how your skills and behavior contributed to the positive outcome.

8. How have you handled angry customers or peers?

The interviewer wants to discern whether you have customer service abilities, so use a specific example in which you utilized the "customer is always right" approach but still protected the interests of the company. If you work in an industry that does not interact directly with customers, you may be asked about how you have handled an angry coworker or difficult situation with a supervisor. The interviewer wants to hear key concepts that tell him or her that you will take personal responsibility for your role, that you will attempt to resolve issues directly with someone else, and that you will seek help if your attempt isn't effective. It's also important to demonstrate that you can remain calm and not get emotional when you face interpersonal challenges.

_____

_____

_____

_____

_____

_____

_____

9. What are your salary expectations?

Salary negotiation depends heavily on the role to which you are applying, your current salary range, and the information you have about the expected salary for the role. If possible, you could begin by asking whether a salary range has been established for the position. If the hiring manager is not willing to offer a range, you should provide information about your current or most recent compensation and then any additional, relevant information (Is the new role a promotion or a step back? Will the new role offer benefits that could outweigh financial compensation such as schedule flexibility or increased vacation? Is the job closer to home?).

Examples: "My prior salary was _XX_ plus benefits. That said, I realize that this position will afford me additional opportunities, so I am open to discussing a slightly lower salary if that number is a little high."

Or

"My prior salary was _XX_. I consider this position to be an increase in responsibility and understand that some evenings and weekends will be required. I would expect an increase over my current earnings to allow for the step up."

_____

_____

_____

_____

_____

_____

_____

10. Do you have any questions?

Always have a few questions prepared and always take notes when you receive these answers. Doing so shows you are interested, that you have done your homework, and that you listened during the interview. However, do *not* ask questions that you could have answered through your own research. Consider making an observation about something you discovered while researching the company and asking whether the interviewer agrees with your observation or finds it to be true in his or her experience.

If the company has been in the news recently, asking questions related to the media coverage can be tricky, especially if the information was negative. However, if the news is pertinent to your position, it is appropriate to ask how the company has been impacted or what the next steps are.

If, however, it was good news—it's great to acknowledge the positive information—ask questions about how this came to pass or to what the company attributes its success.

Worksheet 4: Seven Steps to Prepare for an Interview

Before going to an interview, review the following interview preparation steps to help you get ready. Use this worksheet as a reference for future use and a place to take notes during the workshop.

How to Prepare for an Interview

Step 1: Research the company.

Step 2: Research what kind of interview you will be encountering.

Step 3: Practice mock interviewing.

Step 4: Dress the part.

Step 5: Know where you are going and arrive early.

Step 6: Come prepared.

Step 7: Follow up.

Step 1: Research the Company

You should answer these basic questions for every interview you secure. See **Worksheet 5** for additional detailed information about how to research a company. Additional information is also provided in the Job Search Workshop.

- How long has the company been in business?
- Who founded the company?
- What is the mission statement or company motto?
- How many locations does it have?
- How many employees does it have?

Additional Resources

- Business Week Online
- Hoovers Online
- Forbes Largest Private Companies
- The Inc. 500
- General professional organizations and associations

In addition to basic information, you should know about the company's culture. The following resources may help you find information on the company's culture:

- Company website
- Google—It can provide recent news articles about the company.
- LinkedIn—It may provide you with a list of people who work there and the kind of people the company hires.
- Facebook—It may provide you with insight into the current employees and company social events.
- Twitter—It allows you to follow the company and search for company-related hash tags to see what people are talking about.

Notes: _____

_____

_____

_____

_____

Step 2: Research What Kind of Interview You Will Be Encountering

Because there are many types of interviews, it would be helpful for you to know what kind of interview you will encounter:

- **One-on-one:** This is the most common type of interview. It means you'll be interviewing with the hiring manager or human resources director. You may be asked for a second interview after a one-on-one. Be prepared, however, to have one other person present in this type of interview.

- **Group interview:** In a group interview, you will be interviewed with other candidates. Typically, you will all be asked to answer the same few questions, and you will be given only a small window of time to answer these questions. This is when your newspaper headline style of answering will *really* pay off. If the interviewer asks for a volunteer to go first, speak up! Going first shows initiative, confidence, and a positive attitude. This impression will also help because you will not have to worry about someone else "stealing your thunder." If the interviewer picks the order, do not be discouraged. Give the answers you would give regardless of what others have said and avoid saying "Like 'so-and-so' already said." Just say what you want to say as if it has not been stated previously.

- **Panel interview:** In this type of interview, multiple interviewers will ask you various types of questions. Prepare for this type of interview by role-playing. You will want to keep the entire panel engaged and answer questions as if all of them asked you. Doing so means maintaining eye contact with each panel member. Knowing each person's name and title is also helpful. You should bring something to write on so that you can draw a map and write down their names.

Notes: _____

_____

_____

_____

Step 3: Practice Mock Interviewing

A mock interview is one of the best ways to prepare for an actual employment interview. The mock interview helps you learn what is expected in a real interview and how you can improve the way you present yourself. It is a safe place to practice your interview skills and gain feedback. The following is a list of best practices for mock interviews:

- Record the interview and review it with your partner. The mock interview coach will provide constructive feedback on all aspects of the interview process.

- Make the interview as realistic as possible.

- Use questions from actual employers whenever possible.

- Spend at least 20 minutes on each mock interview; then review and discuss your performance.

- Expect the mock interview and critique to last approximately one hour.

- Focus on how well you know yourself and your past experiences, how well you know the industry you hope to enter, and how well you can convey that information.

- Remember that you will gain the most experience from your mock interview if you treat it like an actual interview.

Notes: _____

_____

_____

_____

Step 4: Dress the Part

Dressing for success is one of the most important parts of an interview. You want to look, act, and smell your best (be clean and wear recently laundered clothing; don't wear perfume at all, but if you feel you must, use it sparingly). If you learn that the company culture is professional casual, dress professionally. *Always* dress up; *never* dress down. Many qualified people have lost out on a job because they were underdressed. Here are some points to consider:

- Locate and have ready one or two interview outfits that you keep cleaned, pressed, and ready to go at all times. A good rule of thumb is to dress one tier more formal than the company dress code. So if the company has a casual dress code, make sure you are in "business casual" attire. If it is business casual, you should wear a comfortable suit or more dressy business outfit.
- Clean and press any button-down shirts (white is best).
- Wear properly fitting clothing.
- It is recommended to wear solid fabrics (no loud or bright prints) in dark colors.
- Cover visible tattoos.
- Remove facial piercings.
- Wear conservative jewelry (women).
- Wear a wrist watch and wedding band (if applicable) for men.
- Do *not* wear cologne or perfume.
- Do not smoke after you have dressed for the interview.
- Unless you are applying for a position in a fashion company, your shoes should not be "attention-grabbing." Wear conservative (low) heels in a dark color, and ensure that they are clean and not overly worn out.

Notes: _____

_____

_____

_____

Step 5: Know Where You Are Going and Arrive Early

It is important to prepare for any obstacle you encounter, so plan ahead and practice driving to the location before the day of your interview. This way, you can identify how long it will take you to arrive as well as identify any road construction or possible obstacles:

- Drive to the interview location at approximately the same time of day as your interview and time yourself.
- Make note of any road construction that may be worse on the day of the interview.
- Use GoogleMaps.com (or other map website) if you need a resource for finding your way.
- Plan to arrive at least 15 minutes early.
- Be ready to go! Interviewers are scheduling their day around you, so if you are waiting in a receiving area, keep your personal belongings neat and together and be ready to go when you are called. Being organized may also provide you the opportunity to make a good impression on the receptionist, whose opinion may be highly valued.

Notes: _____

_____

_____

_____

Step 6: Come Prepared

You need to bring a few items with you on your interview:

- A working black or blue pen
- A completed job application, small day planner, or notebook that contains previous employment information including addresses, phone numbers, contact names, and dates of employment
- Several copies of your resume on linen or other high-quality paper
- A career portfolio including letters of recommendation, references, honors and awards, and education transcripts

Notes: _____

_____

_____

_____

_____

Step 7: Follow Up

Follow up after a job interview in a professional and enthusiastic manner and give the company further proof that you are the right person for the job. Use these steps to follow up successfully after the interview and get the job you want:

- **Find out what happens next.** When closing the interview, ask for information about the next stage in the hiring process. Ask when you may contact the company to find out the status of your application.
- **Get all the necessary contact details.** Make sure you have the full name and title of the interviewer plus his or her contact details.
- **Make notes immediately after the interview.** Make notes on what happened in the job interview as soon as possible.
- **Write and send a thank you letter.** Send a handwritten and relevant thank you letter within 24 hours of the interview. Refer to topics discussed in your interview that will help remind the interviewer why you are a good candidate for the position.
- **Ask for a time to make the follow-up call.** Follow up with a call or email after a couple of days. If you have been given a specific time frame, work within that time frame. Do not wait for the company to contact you.
- **Keep looking.** Continue with your job search—even if you are sure that this is the job for you and you are going to get the offer. It is never wise to rely on just one opportunity.

Notes: _____

_____

_____

_____

Worksheet 5: Research the Company

Research Information

Recall that you should be able to identify two types of company information during your research: tactical information and company culture information. **Tactical information** describes facts that are typically easy to find on the company's website, such as the company's owner, when the company was founded, and what services it offers. **Company culture** describes how a company operates, who it employs, and what is important to the current employees.

This information is relevant to a job seeker for two reasons: (1) it helps you determine whether the job would be a good fit for you (remember, you are also interviewing the employer!) and (2) it helps you identify yourself as someone who would contribute to that culture.

Tactical Questions

This information is typically easy to find on the company website:

- Who owns the company?
- How long has it been in business?
- What are the products and services it offers?
- How many employees does it have, and what is its organizational structure?

Cultural Questions

This information will be more difficult to find. You can talk to current employees, read articles about the company, and refer to the language used on the company website or documents (such as mission statements, values documents, and so on).

1. What types of employees does the company typically hire?
2. If you wanted a job at this company, what would you try to highlight during your interview (skills or otherwise)?

Cultural Resources

- Google—It gives you recent news articles about the company.
- LinkedIn—It gives you a list of people who work there and the kinds of people the company hires.
- Facebook—It tells you a lot about the kinds of people the company hires.
- Twitter—Following the company on Twitter and posting a few comments may be a good idea.

Directions: Apply your understanding of company research by reviewing the information provided in the "Mock Company Information" section and answering the questions that follow.

Mock Company Information: Klutzy Case*

The Company Motto
"We Have Got You Covered!"

About Them
This company is known as innovators of solutions for portable handheld devices. It distributes and sells, direct to the public (via its website), cases for cell phones, e-readers, and tablet computers, to name just a few.

The company was founded in 2001 by James Peterson, a former scientist at the local community college, who still operates as chairman and CEO. He says he built his business on the fundamentals of hard work, creativity, and perseverance. He says the company's cases are dedicated to all the klutzes and those who break their gadgets.

Website Description of Staff Members
A fun, creative bunch that likes to work and play hard. The company has in-house sales, customer service, accounting, engineering, public relations, marketing, web design, graphics, supply chain, manufacturing, and human resources departments, plus its own warehouse. It currently has more than 500 employees at its three locations, which include the warehouse, customer service center, and corporate headquarters.

Company Location
In one of the greatest cities in America—Raleigh, North Carolina. Raleigh shows the cultural graces that go along with anchoring the so-called Research Triangle, home to North Carolina State University, Duke University, and the University of North Carolina at Chapel Hill. Among its many attributes, the city sports 867 restaurants, 110 bars, and 51 museums, as well as a thriving social scene, good schools, and 12,512 park acres.

State-of-the-Art Corporate Headquarters
The headquarters was designed to inspire innovation and to help the Klutzy culture thrive. Created as an exciting and productive atmosphere for staff, this headquarters building contains state-of-the-art offices and executive boardrooms, a coffee bar on the first floor, bike storage, massage room, on-campus gym with state-of-the-art workout gear and locker rooms, interior brick walls, engineered wood walls, special lighting throughout, interior and exterior fireplaces, open spaces, and an outdoor BBQ/patio area on the fourth floor for company meetings and gatherings.

Company Culture
Play hard. Work hard. We are a company focused on developing reliable products, which requires innovative processes to ensure we deliver high-quality products. The people who make this happen are the secret sauce in our success. Collaboration and strategy are something we thrive on and do together. We continually question the way it has always been done and make improvements continuously.

The Company's Description of Employees
Where do you work? Like to work in the dark? Like loud music playing? Like to take your laptop outside on the deck? How about a massage chair break? Maybe a little ping pong or pinball? Like *Star Wars* movies? Rubber band wars? Dancing? Singing? Riding tricycles? Working out at work? If so, you will love working here!

Klutzy Case
Klutzy Case created a nonprofit foundation to formalize its giving efforts. The mission of the foundation is to invest in our community by educating and empowering youth toward positive growth. Through Klutzy Case, all employees are eligible for three full days off for volunteering opportunities.

*Disclaimer: Klutzy Case is not a real company. Any similarities to any real company are strictly coincidental.

Company Tactical Questions

1. How long has the company been in business? _____

2. Who founded the company? _____

3. What is its mission statement or company motto? _____

4. Where is it located? _____

5. What product or services does it provide? _____

6. How many employees does it have? _____

Company Culture Questions

1. What types of employees does the company typically hire? _____

   _____

   _____

   _____

   _____

   _____

2. If you wanted a job at this company, what would you try to highlight during your interview (skills or otherwise)? _____

   _____

   _____

   _____

   _____

   _____

Worksheet 6: Interview Checklist

Make copies of this checklist and gather the information or complete the activities each time you are preparing for an interview. You will be glad to have the information at hand when you are in the interview, and if you are invited back for subsequent interviews, you can refer back to the checklist for this information.

Company Research

Company Name

_____

Details

Write a few sentences here about the company with which you will be interviewing. Include facts and details that may be handy in your interview:

_____

_____

_____

_____

_____

_____

1. What kind of interview should I expect?

   _____

   _____

2. What is the company dress code?

   _____

3. What will I wear?

   _____

   _____

   _____

The Week before My Interview

Arrange to complete a mock interview (if you can't do a mock interview with someone, run through **Worksheet 3: Most-Asked Interview Questions** and practice your answers in front of a mirror.

Date of mock interview: _____

Location: _____

Day before My Interview/Getting There on Time

Practice driving to the location of the interview (preferably at the same time you would be driving to your actual interview) and note any obstacles you encountered:

_____

_____

Address of the Interview

_____

_____

How long did it take to get there? _____

With whom will you be meeting? _____

Do you need parking information?   Y / N

Are there any special instructions for accessing the building? _____

Day of My Interview

1. What day is my interview? _____

2. What time is my interview? _____

3. How long will it take to get there? _____

4. What time must I leave for my interview? (Add 30 minutes to the preceding time to allow for any unforeseen obstacles.) _____

5. What should I take with me?

   ☐ Note paper

   ☐ Pencil or pen

   ☐ Notes from my research

   ☐ A list of questions to ask if there is time

   ☐ Copies of my resume

   ☐ Portfolio or examples of my work and letters of reference

   ☐ Blank thank you notes, envelopes, and stamps (You can write your thank you note immediately after finishing and drop it in the mail near the building where you interviewed.)

6. Is any additional follow-up necessary?

_____

_____

PASSPORT to CAREER SUCCESS

INTERNSHIPS
Make Your Experience Count

Worksheet 1: The VIP Approach

Directions: Follow along with the workshop facilitator and complete the following sentences to identify the three key parts of the VIP approach to internships. When you are finished, record any additional notes in the space that follows.

V   Have a _____ for your internship.

I   Gather _____ that you will need to be successful.

P   _____ to become an indispensable member of the team at your internship site.

Workshop Notes

_____

_____

_____

_____

_____

_____

_____

_____

_____

_____

_____

_____

_____

_____

_____

_____

_____

_____

_____

Worksheet 2: The Goal of Internships

Directions: Fill in the following information based on the workshop discussion. First, identify the purpose of an internship. Next, record ways to achieve this goal in the To-Do List that follows; use ideas from the workshop discussion.

Internship ➜ _____

To-Do List

_____

_____

_____

_____

_____

_____

_____

_____

_____

_____

_____

_____

_____

_____

_____

_____

_____

_____

_____

_____

_____

_____

Worksheet 3: Expectations during Your Internship

Internship Expectations

Directions: Fill in the following information based on the workshop discussion and presentation.

1. Complete all required _____.

2. _____ to the job site _____ to the first day.

3. _____ the night before.

4. Check in _____ with Career Services (if available).

5. Expect your first week to be _____.

6. Do not be _____ for any reason.

7. Have a _____ voicemail message.

8. Under no circumstances are you to _____ an internship.

9. Take _____.

10. Ask _____ when you do not _____.

11. Follow _____.

12. Call your _____ [and _____] if you are going to be _____.

13. Have a _____ attitude _____ day.

14. Ask for and welcome _____ or _____.

Worksheet 4: Indispensable Team Member

Directions: Write the characteristics of great team players and "indispensable" employees in the spaces provided.

1. Understand their _____ and play it _____

2. Follow _____

3. Ask good _____

4. Take _____

5. Wait their _____

6. Help others when they _____

7. _____ to others

8. Are _____ of their role

Worksheet 5: Self-Assessment — How Prepared Do You Feel?

Name: _____

Email address: _____

Contact phone number: _____

Directions: The purpose of this self-assessment form is to assess what you have learned and determine how confident you feel about starting your internship.

Using the following scale, rate yourself based on what you learned in the workshop. Then, for any area that you rate a 2 or a 3, write down several ways that you can sharpen those skills. When you are finished, please turn in this form to your course facilitator.

> Rating Scale
> 1. I feel very confident about my skills and abilities in this area.
> 2. My skills are OK in this area.
> 3. I have room for improvement in this area.

Evaluation Area	Rate Yourself			Comments
Technical skills needed at the externship	1	2	3	
Professionalism skills needed at the externship	1	2	3	
My ability to become an integral part of the team	1	2	3	
My ability to identify my role on the team	1	2	3	
My life circumstances (transportation, child care, etc.)	1	2	3	

Things I Can Do to Improve

_____

_____

_____

_____

_____

_____

_____

Things I Learned from This Workshop

_____

_____

_____

_____

_____

_____

_____

Concerns I Still Have about My Internship

_____

_____

_____

_____

_____

_____

_____